Mel Bay's
ukulele m
FOR CHORD AND MELC
by Roy Smeck

ROY SMECK, Wizard of the Strings

Roy Smeck is the foremost authority on the ukulele in the United States today. He has been writing for the uke since 1928. He has made over 500 recordings and has appeared throughout the world at leading concert halls and on radio and TV. It is with great pleasure that we present Roy's own method for playing the ukulele. His thorough and comprehensive approach is presented here in this text. Roy has been a personal friend of mine for many years, and I, too, have the pleasure of calling him the "Wizard of the Strings".

Author's Note: My thanks to Richard Pearl for his help in proofreading.

The Ukulele

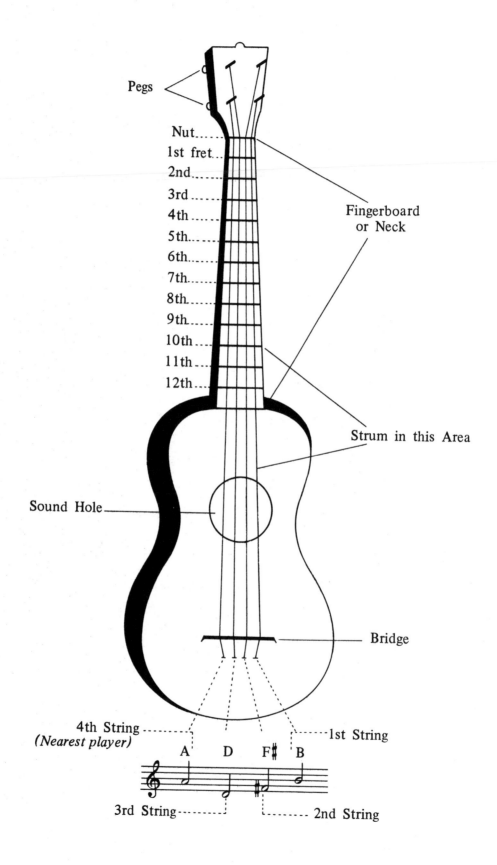

Notes Found on Ukulele Fingerboard

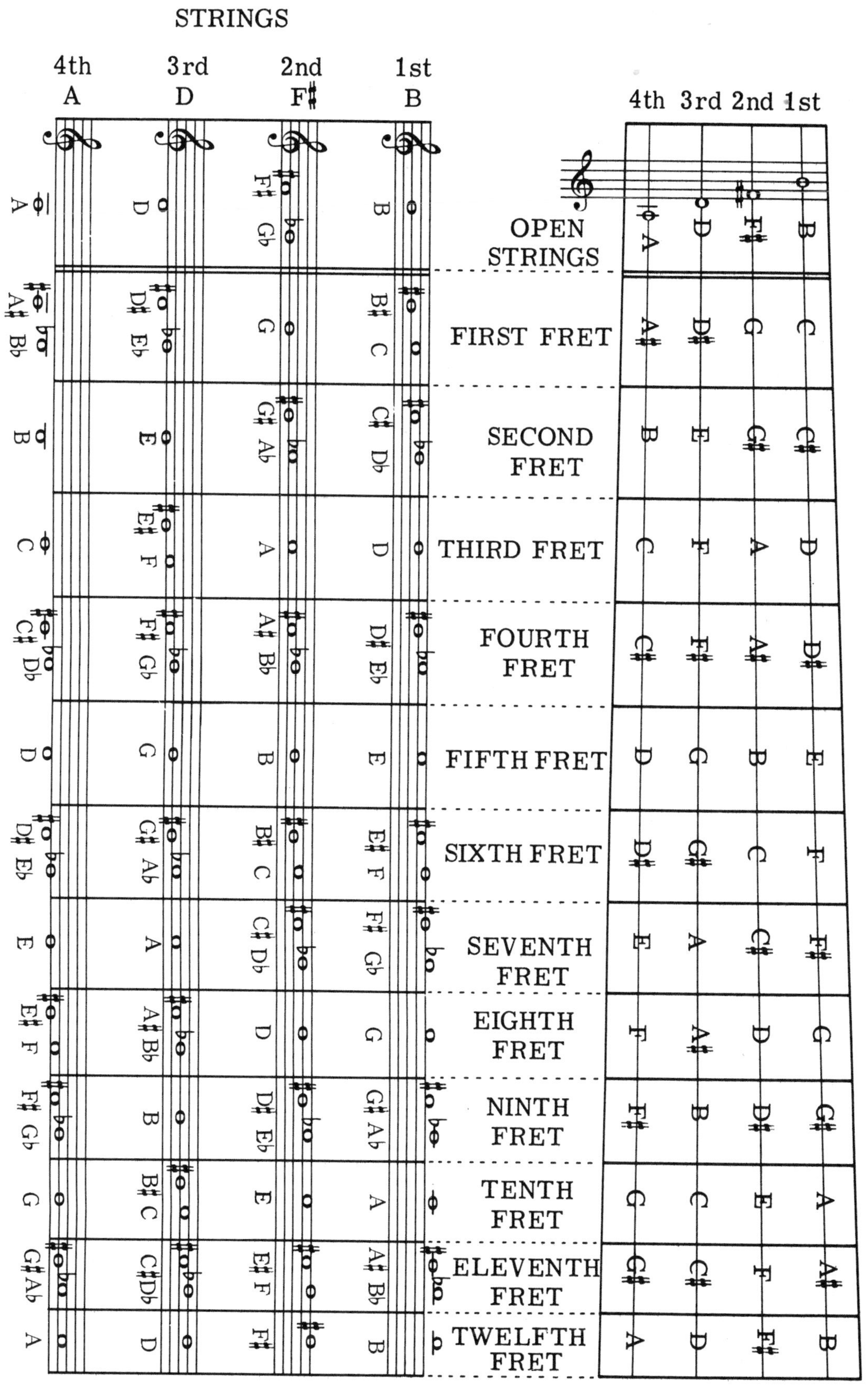

How to Tune the Ukulele

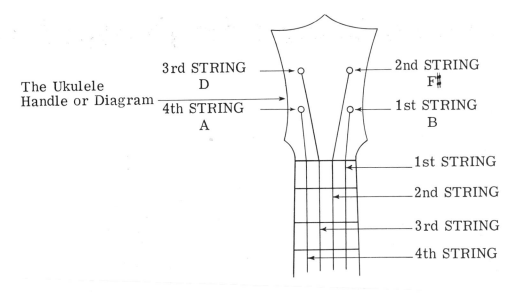

The Ukulele
Handle or Diagram

3rd STRING D

4th STRING A

2nd STRING F♯

1st STRING B

1st STRING

2nd STRING

3rd STRING

4th STRING

Piano Keyboard

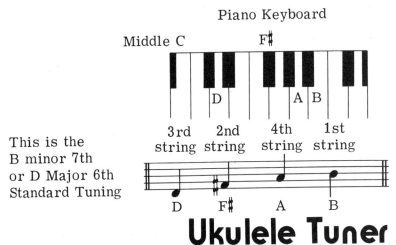

Middle C

F♯

D — 2nd string

A — 4th string

B — 1st string

3rd string — D

This is the
B minor 7th
or D Major 6th
Standard Tuning

D   F♯   A   B

Ukulele Tuner

The Ukulele Tuner way is the easiest way to tune.
You just blow the sound on the Tuner and tune each string to the sound.

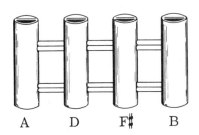

A   D   F♯   B

HOW TO TUNE THE UKULELE WITHOUT PIANO OR TUNER

(1) Tune the 3rd string D to a tone not too low nor too high, then press the finger right behind the 4th fret of this string and tune 2nd string to this sound;
(2) Then press the finger behind the 5th fret of the 2nd string and tune the 1st string to this sound.
(3) Now press the finger behind the 3rd fret of the 2nd string and tune the 4th string to that sound.

Now the instrument is tuned and the tuning tones are: A-4th string;
D-3rd string;   F♯(sharp) — 2nd string and B - 1st string.

If you remember the old way of tuning by ear, the old saying "My Dog Has Fleas" will do the job. If you don't know, ask your friends. They might remember.

Picking the Strings on the Ukulele

FINGER STYLE

Start strumming with the index finger of the right hand. That means the finger after the thumb. Leave your finger loose and just strike down and up on the strings.

OR

With a Ukulele Felt Pick

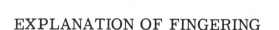

EXPLANATION OF FINGERING

Numerals alongside of the black dots indicate left hand fingers to be placed directly behind the frets:

1 = index finger

2 = middle finger

3 = ring finger

Zeros (0) signify open strings - not to be fingered.

Hint about Your Ukulele

Did you know there is a little secret that might help prevent your ukulele strings from slipping? Turn your ukulele around, now you are looking at its back. Now - then, see the little pegs on the top? In the middle of each peg you'll find a tiny screw. Take a thin knife, or better still, a metal nail file and tighten each screw. You'll find this a good prevention for slipping strings.

Rudiments of Music

It is necessary that the student should be acquainted with musical notation.

The relative value of the notes is best shown by the following arrangement:
Notes are divided into Bars by single or double lines drawn across the stave.

One line ≣ is placed after each bar. Each bar contains the same number or value of notes, and must last precisely the same length of time.

Seven characters determine the value of notes, seven the value of rests.

Forms of Different Notes and Rests

A Dot placed after any note increases its value one half, Thus:

Comparative Table
Showing the Relative Value of Notes

1. Whole Note
   equals
2. Half Notes
   equals
4. Quarter Notes
   equals
8. Eighth Notes
   equals
16. Sixteenth Notes
   and so on.

Explanation of
Ukulele Diagrams

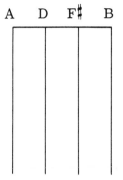

The four vertical
lines represent
the strings.

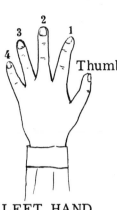

LEFT HAND

1 - Index finger
2 - 2nd finger
3 - 3rd finger
4 - 4th finger

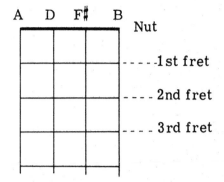

The horizontal lines represent
the frets or tone spaces. Each
fret has a musical value of one-
half tone.

The black dots designate the strings to be pressed. Strings without dots are open and should be played unless marked otherwise.

Numbers next to dots indicate which finger of the left hand should press the string.

Strings

4th 3rd 2nd 1st

Example 1

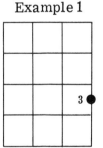

press finger tightly
on the string in the
space between the
frets.

Example 2

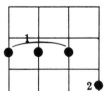

1st finger may be
placed over all
the strings.

Example 3

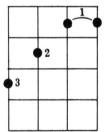

1st finger should press
1st and 2nd string.

Example 4

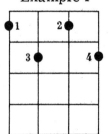

Tilt wrist to left
and arch all fingers.

"DON'T FORGET"

Where more than one string is pressed with one finger, a bracket is used to indicate it;⌒

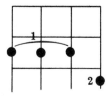

The following strokes may be practiced on all chord exercises. Be sure to practice slowly After a while you can make up your own strokes. Try the easy chords first, etc.

Strokes

The Common Stroke

This is the most popular stroke, and the only one that beginners should use until they have mastered the chord fingering and changing with the left hand. With the first finger of the right hand, strike downward over all the strings with the back of the nail, and come up again with the flesh of the finger tip. Do not use the side of the finger nail, as it will produce a rough sound. Down and up are counted as one beat.

Do this four times in every measure of music written in common time or $\frac{4}{4}$ time. Do this three times in every measure of music written in waltz time or $\frac{3}{4}$ time.

An arrow with the index pointing downward will be used to indicate the down stroke, and an arrow with the index pointing upward will indicate the up stroke.

Common stroke written and played thus: —

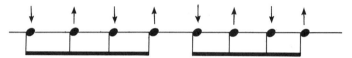

The Syncopated Stroke

Also known as the "Beach Boy Stroke"

This is played by varying the down and up strokes like this:

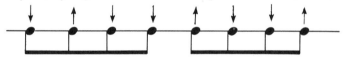

This stroke is also done with the 1st finger of the right hand.

The Triplet Stroke

Also known as the "Hula a Stroke"

With the first finger of the right hand follow these arrow indications carefully.

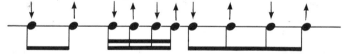

The Roll Stroke

First play a down and up stroke with the 1st finger.

Now be sure to loosen *all* your fingers and (starting with the 4th finger) pass over all the strings with one finger at a time, ending with the thumb.

This does not however complete the stroke. After you have done this, *Finish* by playing up, down, up, with the 1st finger only, which completes the roll stroke.

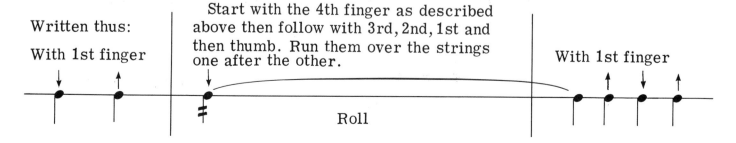

Written thus:

With 1st finger

Start with the 4th finger as described above then follow with 3rd, 2nd, 1st and then thumb. Run them over the strings one after the other.

With 1st finger

Roll

Novelty Professional Strokes

No. 1. THE CIRCLE STROKE   No. 2. THE FIGURE 8 STROKE

No. 3. THE ZIGZAG STROKE

Use a Felt pick or the INDEX FINGER of your right hand,(that is the first finger after thumb.)

EXPLANTION

No. 1. THE ROUND AND ROUND THE CIRCLE STROKE

The Ukulele Body below is laid out from left to right just the way you hold the Ukulele. To make sure you understand what we mean, place the Ukulele on top of the Illustration showing the Ukulele below. Now follow the arrows for the Circle Stroke. Notice that it is done around and around the Hole of the Ukulele.

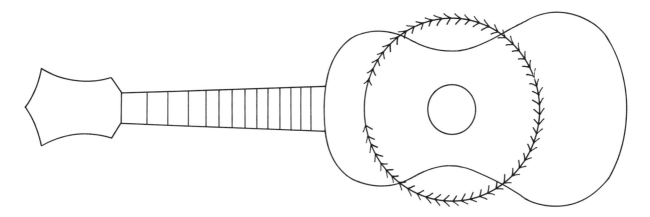

Keep practicing Round and Around the Hole.

The Figure Eight Stroke

No. 2. The Figure Eight Stroke is a very effective stroke producing a fine rhythm and sound. Practice slow at first - See Ex. - of the layout of the Ukulele before you start. Follow arrows throughout the movement, continue on until you have memorized the stroke.

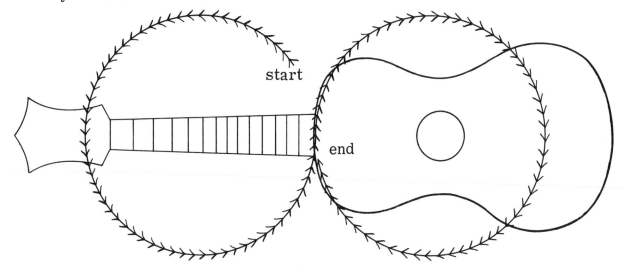

When you reach the End, go to Start again.

The Zigzag Stroke

No. 3. THE ZIGZAG STROKE is done as follows:

Always follow the arrows.

This is strictly a Down and Up stroke starting from the fingerboard or Handle to the Hole of the Body, back and forth.

Start down

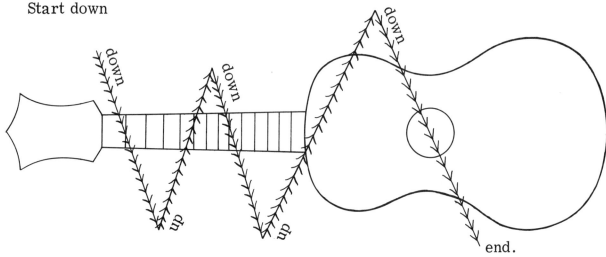

Try to squeeze in as many down and up strokes as possible, the more the more effective. Always go to the starting point, when you reach the end.

Total Tonal Range of Normal 12 fret Uke with $\boxed{D}$ Tuning A D F♯ B

SCALES

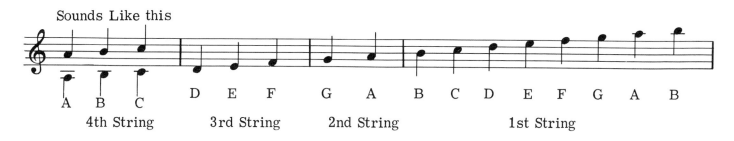

Sounds Like this

A B C | D E F | G A B C | D E F G A B

4th String   3rd String   2nd String   1st String

$\boxed{D}$ Major Scale

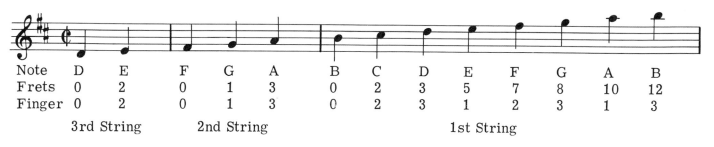

Note	D	E	F	G	A	B	C	D	E	F	G	A	B
Frets	0	2	0	1	3	0	2	3	5	7	8	10	12
Finger	0	2	0	1	3	0	2	3	1	2	3	1	3

3rd String   2nd String   1st String

0 Means open String 1-2-3 Means which finger to use.

$\boxed{D}$ in Scale Diagram form Frets are Marked 1-2-3-4 up to 12

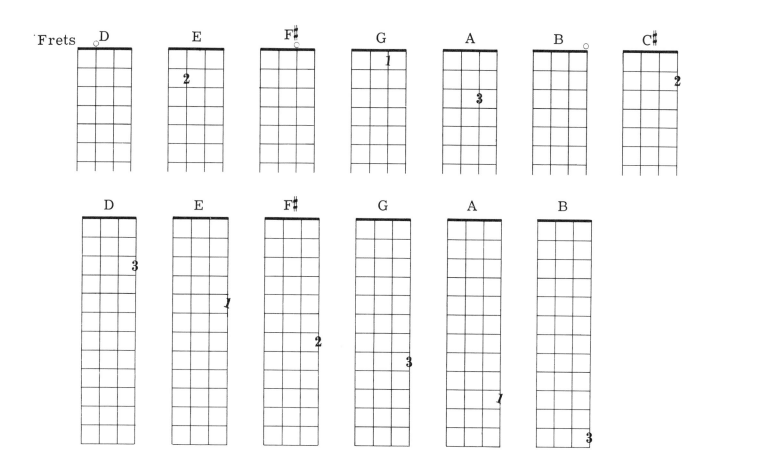

Movable Scale Patterns

Illustrated in diagram form for simplicty, this pattern will allow student to play
all scales by moving up and down the fingerboard following the same pattern.

Finger the dots as shown. (Major Scales) Eb scale

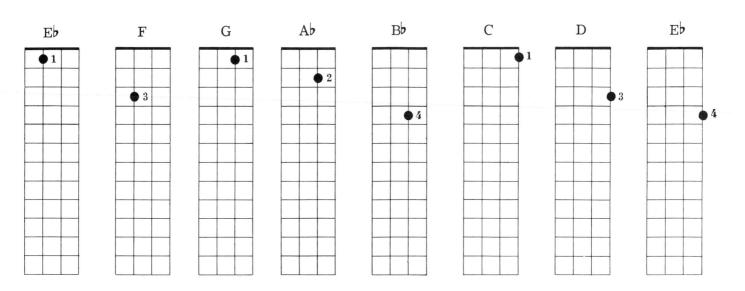

The G Scale

Open string

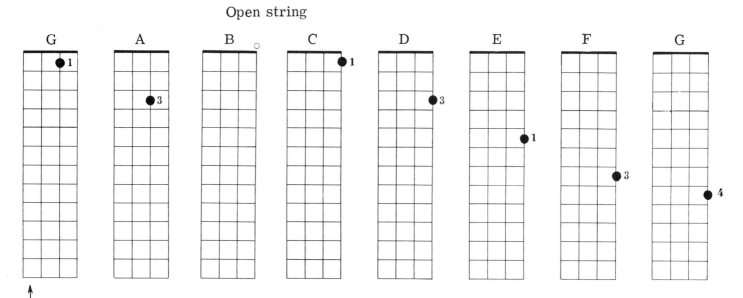

This scale is presented G so that the student may take advantage of the lower fuller
sounding notes derived from the second or F# string. This scale can also be played using
the movable scale pattern by starting on the fifth fret of the third D string.

How to Play the Following Musical Selections

The system of musical notation used will allow both the reader and non-reader of music to master any of the following songs.

1st - Those students only interested in <u>chordal accompaniment</u> will find the appropriate chord symbols and fingering given <u>above the musical score.</u>

2nd - Those students interested in playing the <u>melody of the songs</u> in their entirety will find the diagram method presented <u>below the musical score</u> an ideal teacher. Practice these diagrams just as given and you will find that you shall indeed be playing the melody of the song in a chordal structure right on the uke.

To play the lower diagrams the following instructions should be followed;

a) Start by using the thumb of your right hand-more sophisticated strokes can be used once you're sure of where the melody lies and what effects you desire.

b) The uke fingerboard is presented in a diagram form.
The numbers correspond to the fret numbers and the vertical lines to the strings.

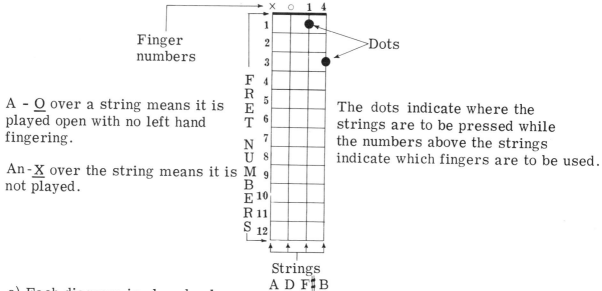

Finger numbers

A - <u>O</u> over a string means it is played open with no left hand fingering.

An -<u>X</u> over the string means it is not played.

The dots indicate where the strings are to be pressed while the numbers above the strings indicate which fingers are to be used.

Strings
A D F♯ B

c) <u>Each</u> diagram <u>is</u> <u>played</u> <u>only</u> <u>once.</u>

d) Start with a familiar melody and take just the 1st part of the song.
Listen to the melody as you carefully find the various left hand positions while using the thumb of the right hand to "<u>pluck</u> <u>out</u> <u>the</u> <u>melody.</u>"
When you feel somewhat comfortable with what you have played, take the next part of the song-and so on until you have played the entire piece.

When you feel comfortable with the left hand fingerings, try playing in a steady tempo, <u>not</u> <u>too</u> <u>fast</u>, until you're satisfied with the way the song sounds. Finally, you can start improving right hand strokes to make the song sound even more unique.

Little Brown Jug

TRADITIONAL

Down in the Valley

TRADITIONAL

Sidewalks of New York
(East side West side)

C. LAWLOR
J. BLAKE

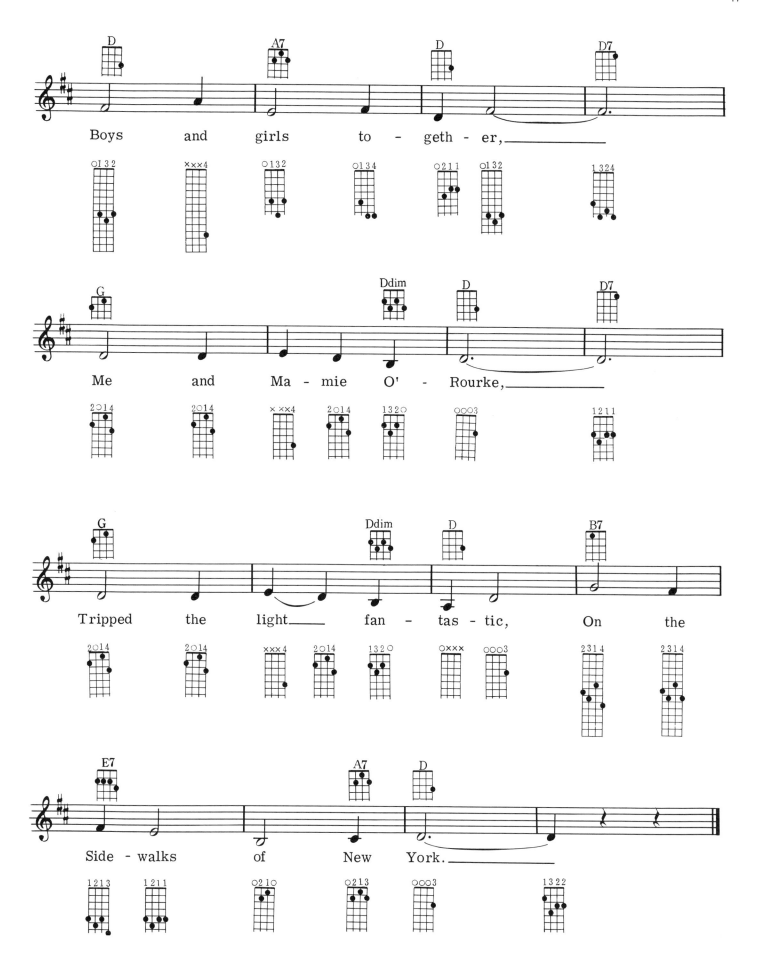

Bicycle Built for Two
(Daisy Bell)

H. DACRE

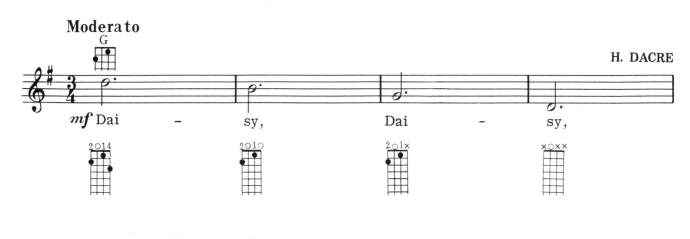

Moderato

mf Dai - sy, Dai - sy,

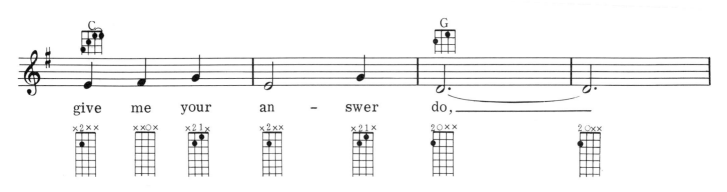

give me your an - swer do, ____

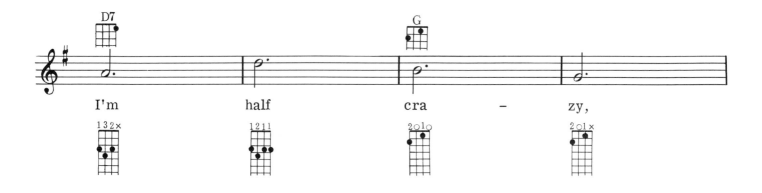

I'm half cra - zy,

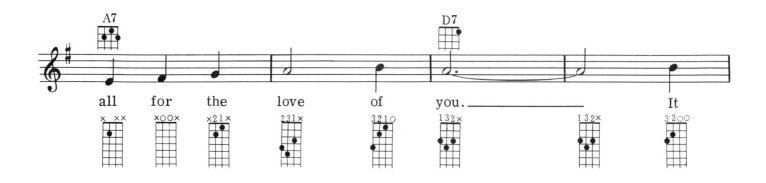

all for the love of you. ____ It

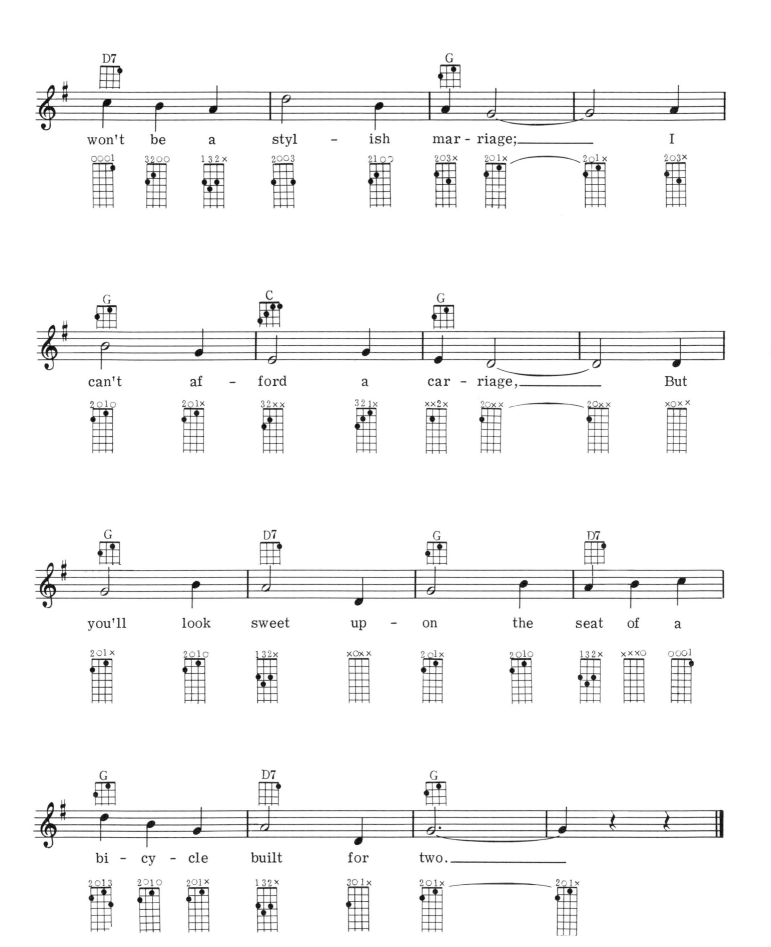

In the Good Old Summer Time

Words by R. SHIELDS
Music by G. EVANS

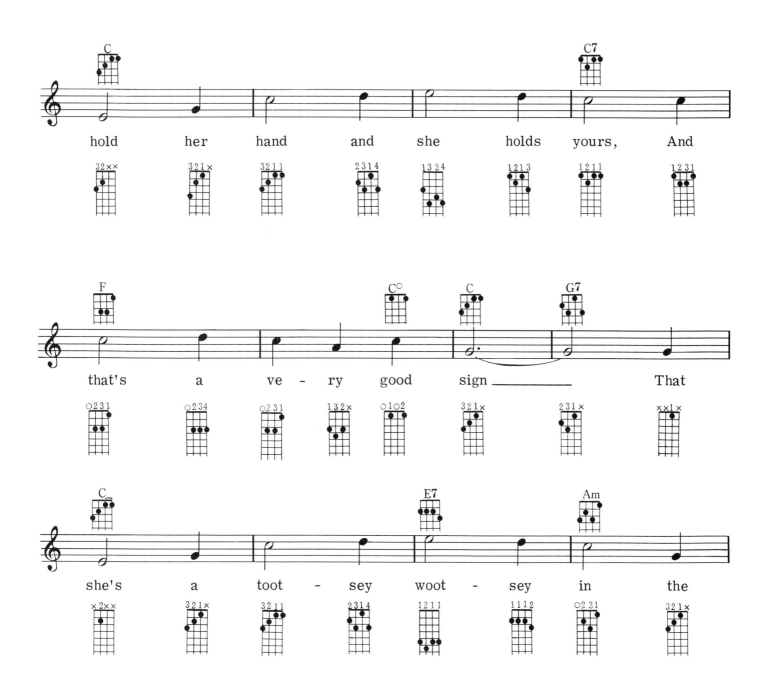
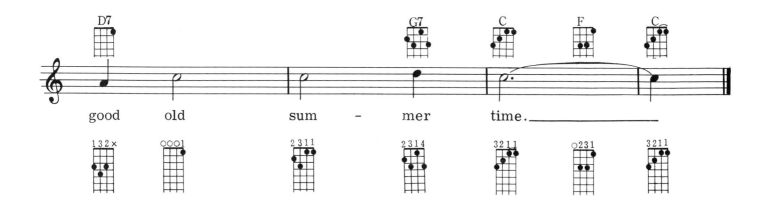

Oh! Susanna

STEPHEN C. FOSTER

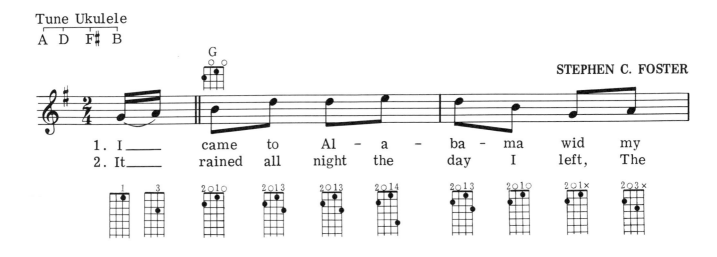

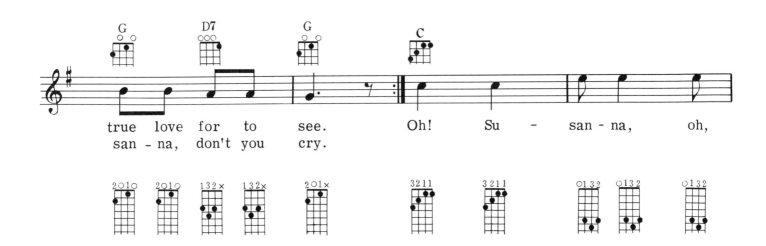

23

Tom Dooley

TRADITIONAL

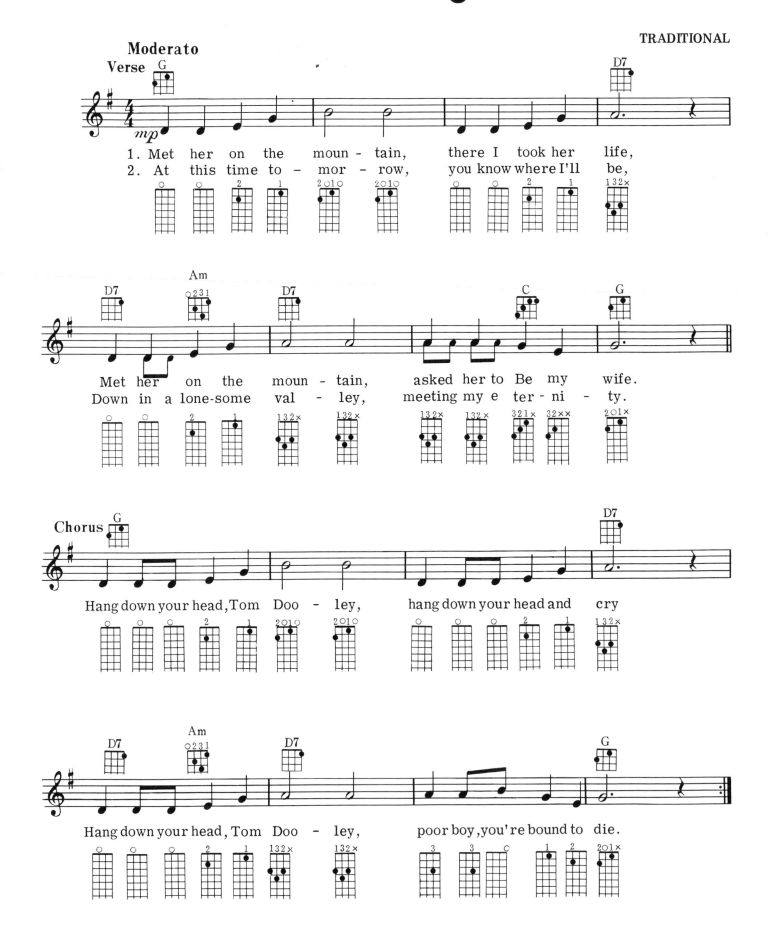

PART II
THE CHORD FAMILIES

C Major

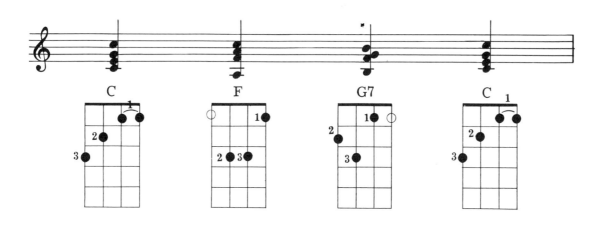

Exercises

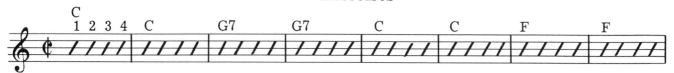

A Minor

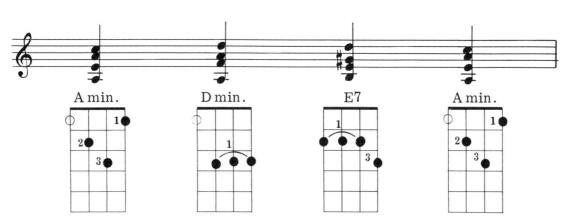

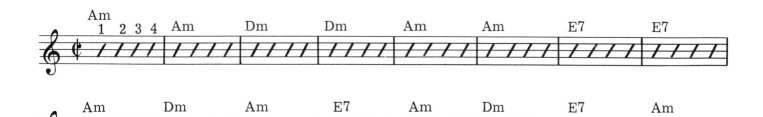

G Major

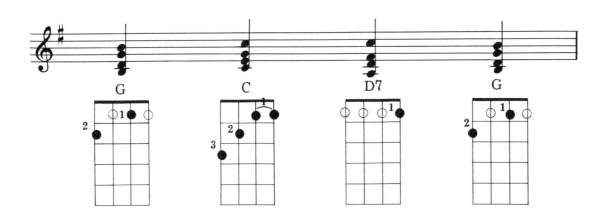

Exercises

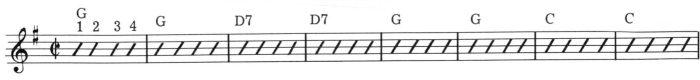

E Minor

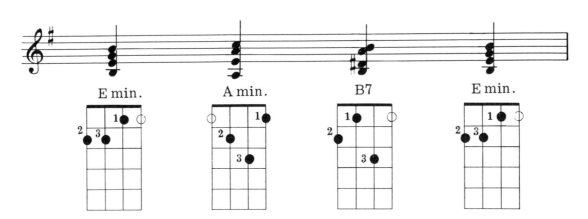

Exercises

D Major

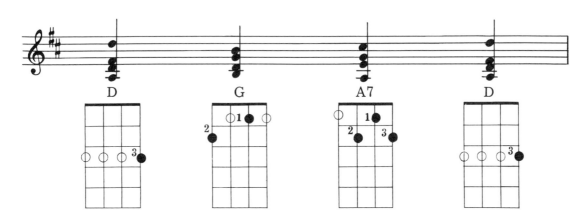

Exercises

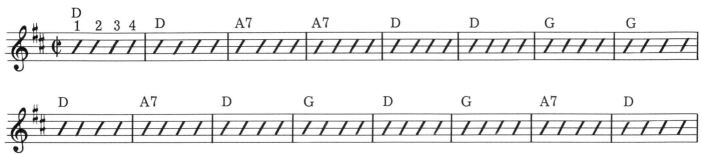

B Minor

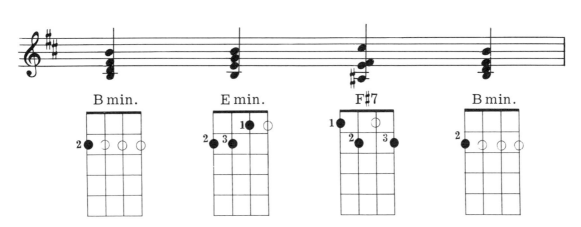

Exercises

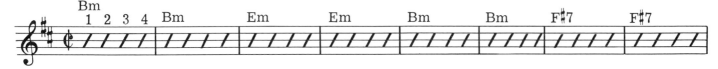

A Major

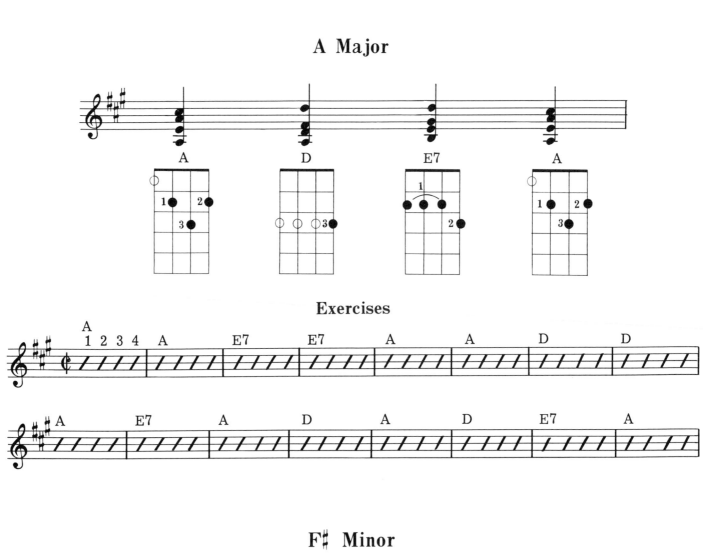

Exercises

F♯ Minor

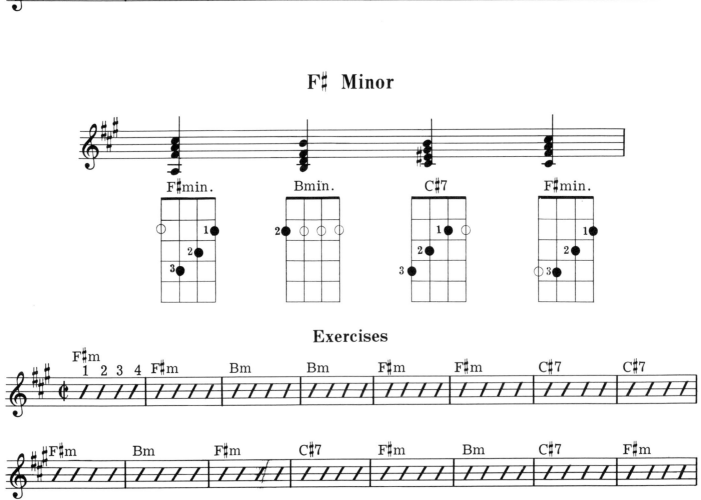

Exercises

E Major

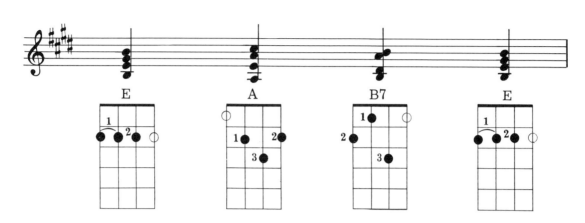

Exercises

C♯ Minor

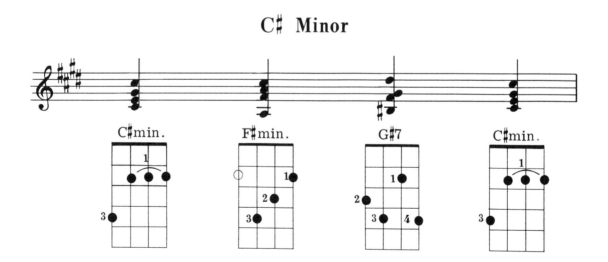

Exercises

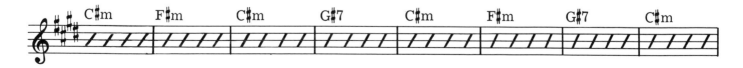

B Major

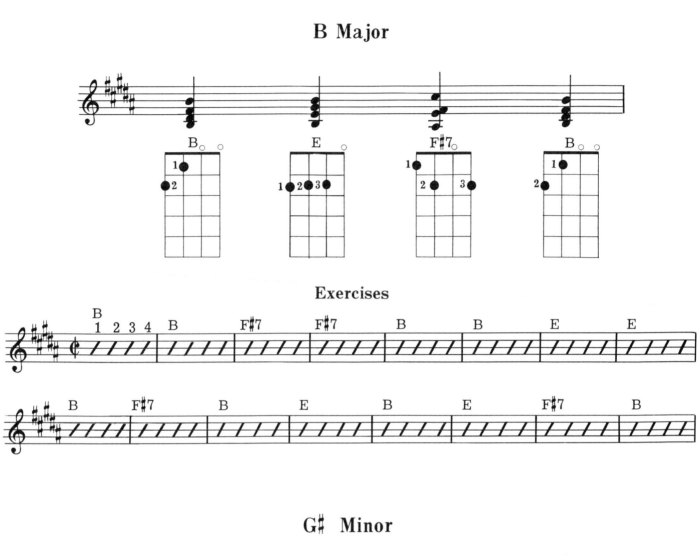

Exercises

G♯ Minor

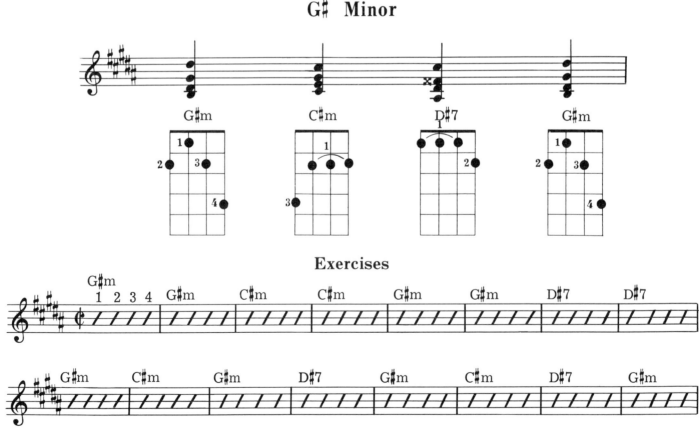

Exercises

G♭ Major-Six Flats or F♯ Major-Six Sharps
G♭ Major

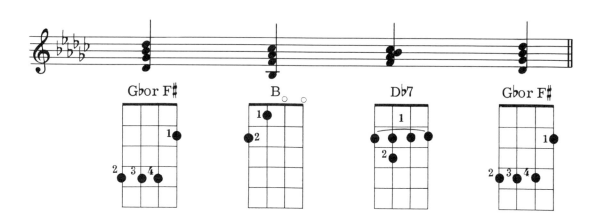

Exercises

E♭ Minor

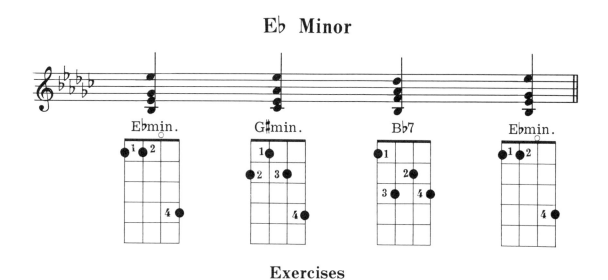

Exercises

F Major

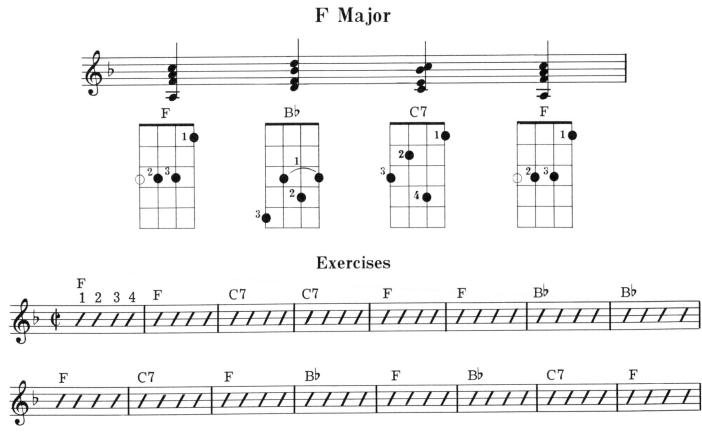

D Minor

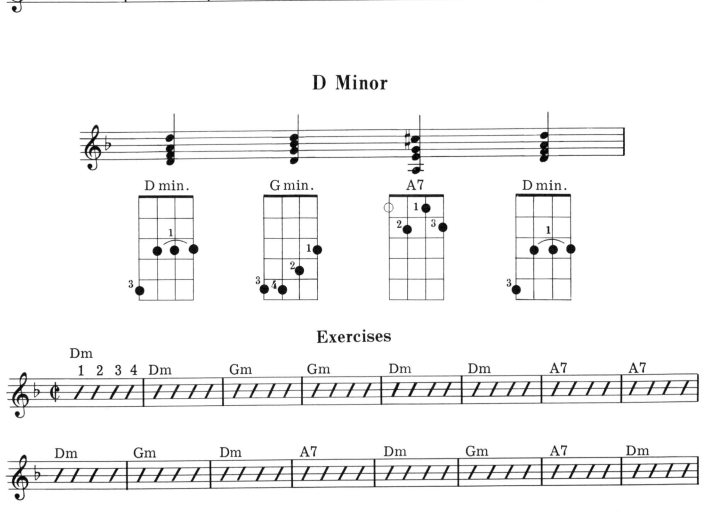

B♭ Major

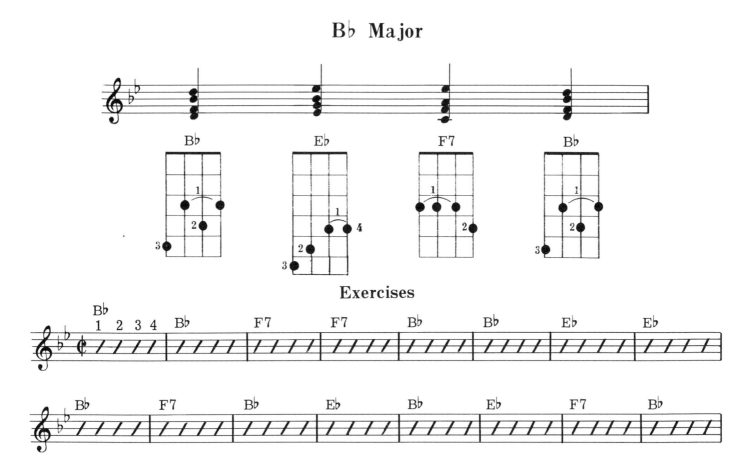

Exercises

G Minor

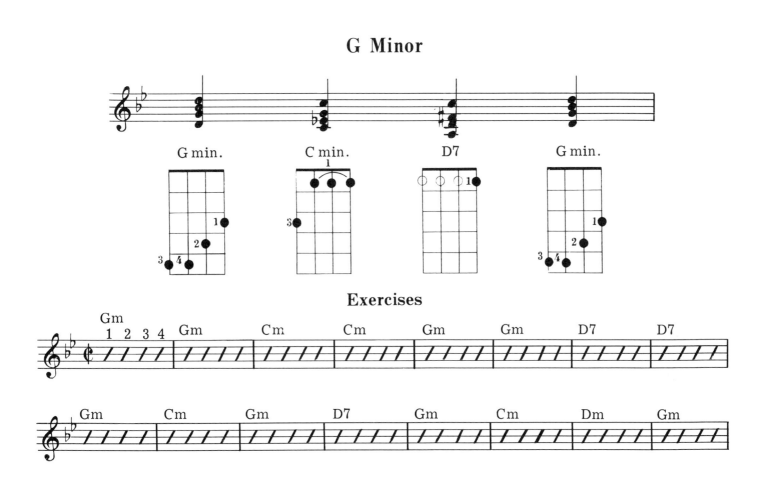

Exercises

E♭ Major

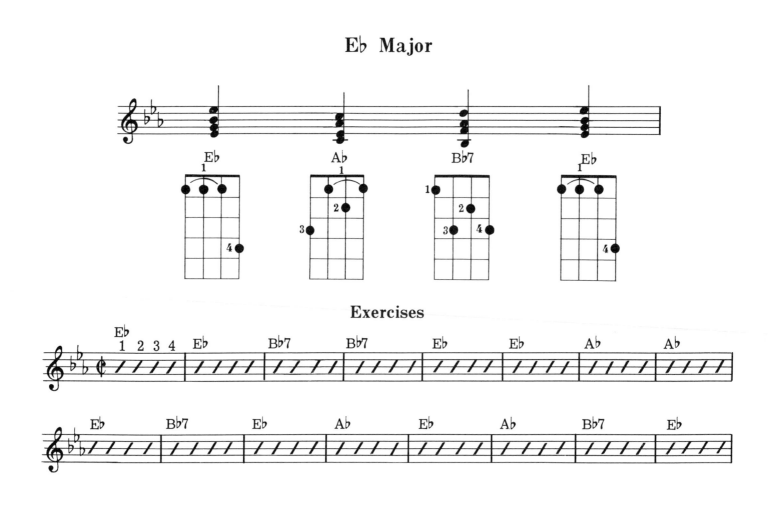

Exercises

C Minor

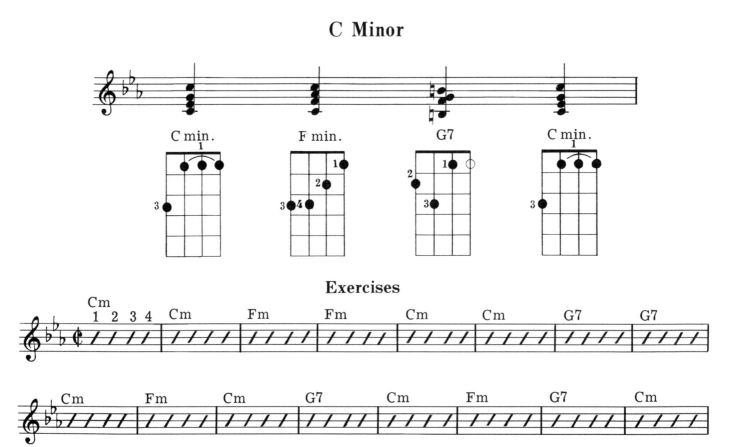

Exercises

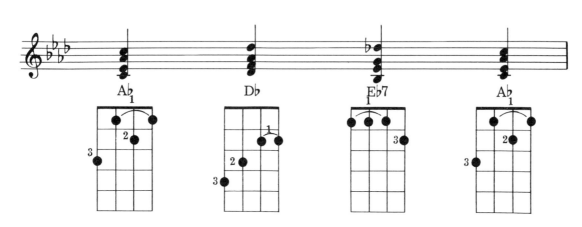

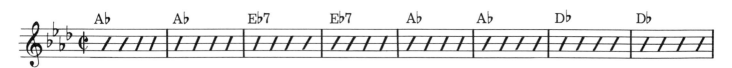

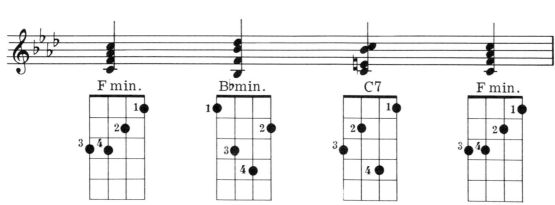

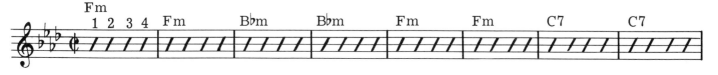

Db Major

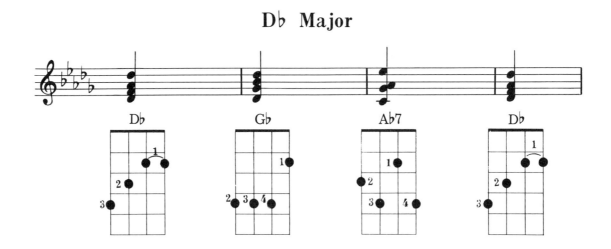

Exercises

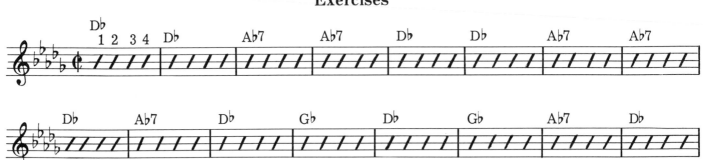

Bb Minor

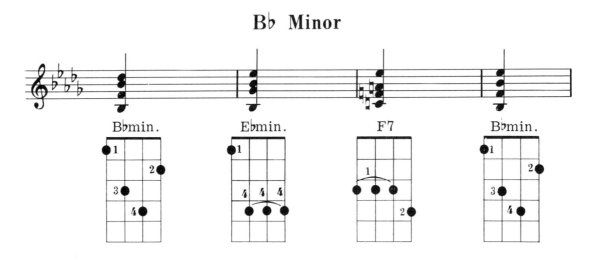

Exercises

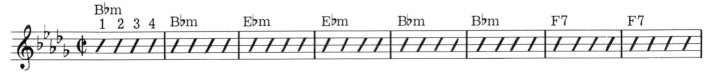

Introductions and Endings
Play Each Diagram Twice-Slowly

Here are some of favorite intros and endings. Play each diagram twice and slowly with two strums or pickings.

I have used these intros and endings in my uke albums. - I have arranged them in all keys. Hope you like them.

Intro's Key of C

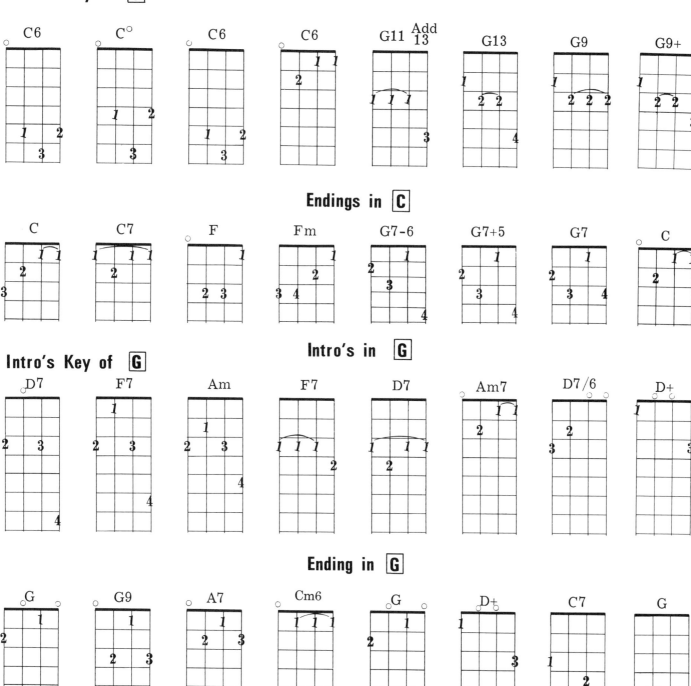

Endings in C

Intro's Key of G

Intro's in G

Ending in G

38

Intro's in the Key of D

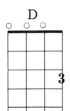
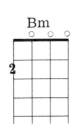
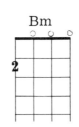
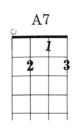
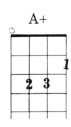

Ending in the Key of D

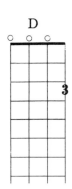

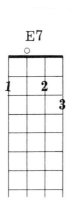
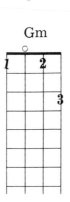

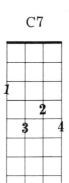
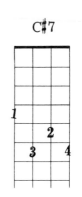
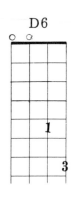

Intro's in the Key of A

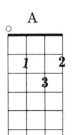
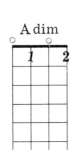
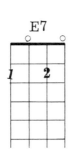
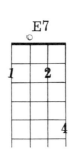
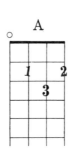
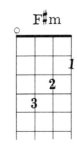

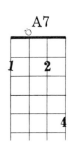

Ending in the Key of A

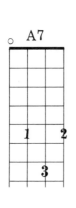
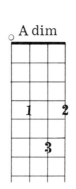
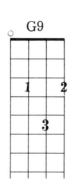

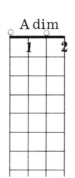
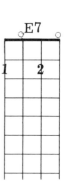

Introduction in the Key of F

 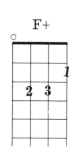 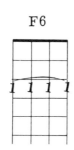 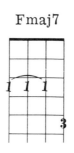 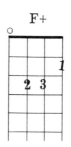 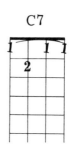 

Ending in the Key of F

 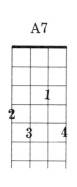 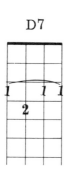  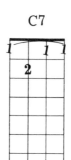  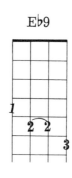 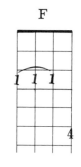

Introduction in the Key of E

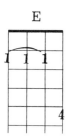 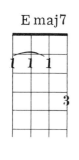 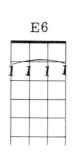   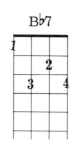 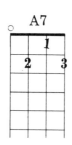 

Ending in the Key of E

 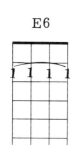 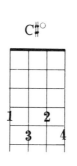  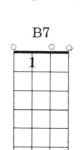 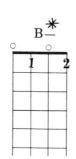 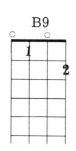 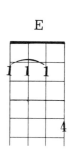

— = Diminished Chord

Introduction in the Key of B

B	B dim	F#7	F#7+	F	B dim	F#9	F#9+

 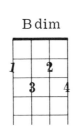 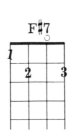 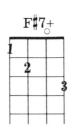 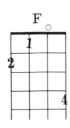  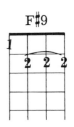 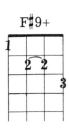

Ending in the Key of B

B maj7	C dim	B6	B dim	B	F#7	F#7+	B

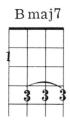     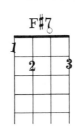 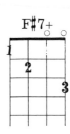 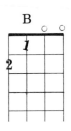

Introduction in the Key of F#

F#	G dim	C#9	C#9+	F#6	D7	C#7	C#+

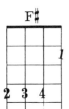  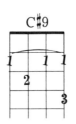 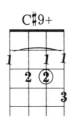 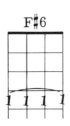 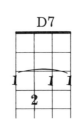  

Ending in the Key of F#

F#	F#7	B7	D7	F#	F#dim	C#9	F#

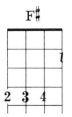 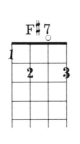 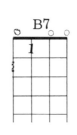 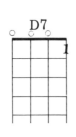 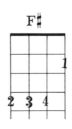  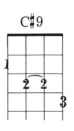 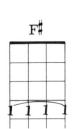

Introduction in the Key of Bb

Bb	Bbdim	F7	F7+	Bb	F dim	F7	F+

 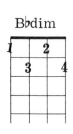 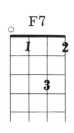 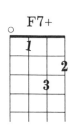 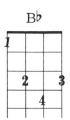 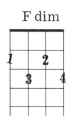 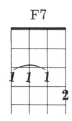 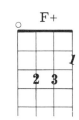

Endings in the Key of Bb

Bb	Bb7	EbM6	Bb	Bb	F7	Bb7/6	Bb6

 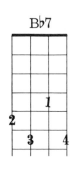 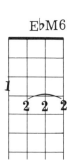  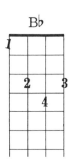  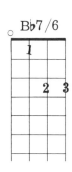 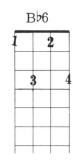

Introducing in the Key of Eb

Eb6	Eb	E maj7	Eb6	Ebdim	Ebdim	Ebdim	Bb7

 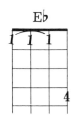 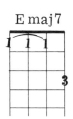  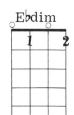 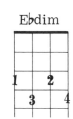 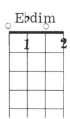 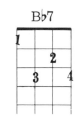

Ending in the Key of Eb

Eb	Eb	Eb7	Eb7	Bb7b9	Bb7b9	Eb6	Ebmaj7

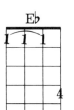  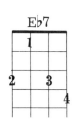 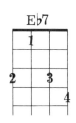  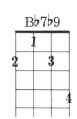  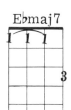

Introduction in the Key of Ab

| Ab | Eb° | Db6 | Eb7 | Ab | Eb° | Eb9 | Eb+ |

 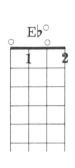 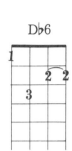  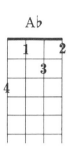  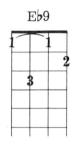 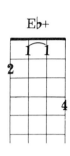

Ending in the Key of Ab

| Ab | Ab7 | Db | Dbm6 | Ab | Db7 | Eb6 | Ab6 |

    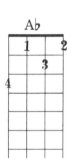 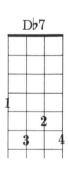 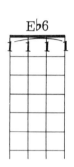 

Introduction in the Key of Db

| D6 | Db6 | Gb6 | Ab9 | Db | Abdim | Ab7 | Ab7+ |

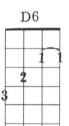 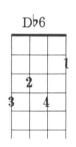  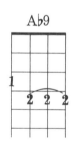    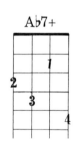

Ending in the Key of Db

| Db | Db7 | Gb | Gbm | Db | Ab7+ | Ab7 | Db6 |

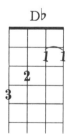  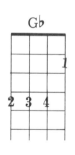  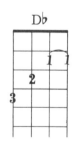 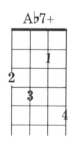  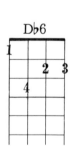

These are the principle inversions for the most used chords. The advanced student would do well to memorize as many of these as possible - They make melody playing (playing the melody of a song in the chords) a snap.

Practice each key - from top to bottom of the page - & back again. Then try substituting these advanced positions for those already known. You'll be amazed at the different possible combinations attainable!

Practice major positions first. You'll notice that similar patterns will evolve. These patterns will help you remember the various positions.

Once the major chords are familiar, go on to the minor positions - and so on- Good Luck!

Positions for Major Chords

1st POSITION

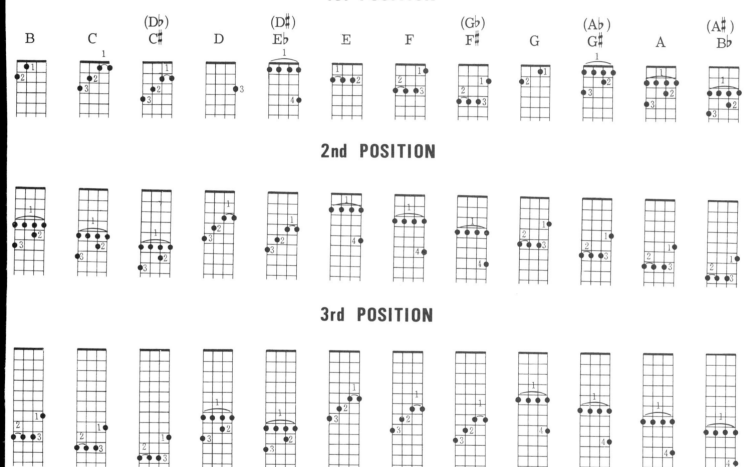

2nd POSITION

3rd POSITION

Positions for Diminished Seventh Chords

1st POSITION

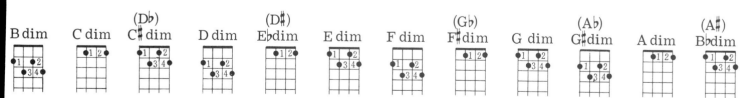

This one's easy - it just repeats every 4th fret - try it - play B dim as shown -now start on the fret 4th - it sounds the same - just a little higher pretty nice huh!!

Positions for Minor Chords

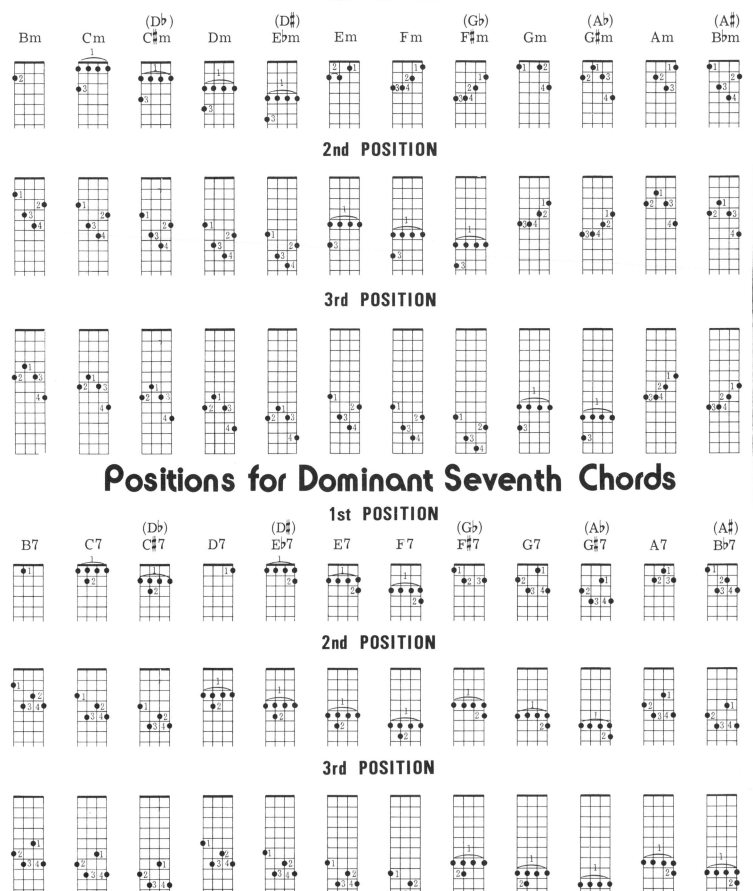

Positions for Dominant Seventh Chords

Positions for Dominant Ninth Chords

1st POSITION

2nd POSITION

3rd POSITION

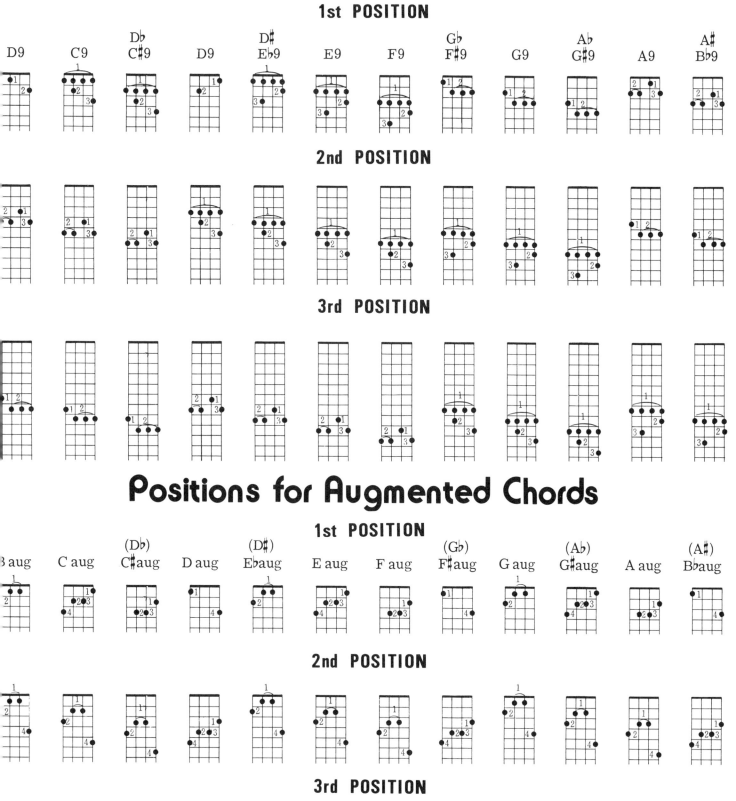

Positions for Augmented Chords

1st POSITION

2nd POSITION

3rd POSITION

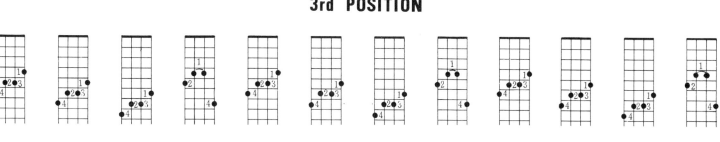

46

Positions for
DOMINANT SEVENTH CHORDS WITH RAISED FIFTH(7th+5)
1st POSITION

2nd POSITION

3rd POSITION

Positions for
DOMINANT SEVENTH CHORDS WITH LOWERED FIFTH(7th−5)
1st POSITION

2nd POSITION

3rd POSITION

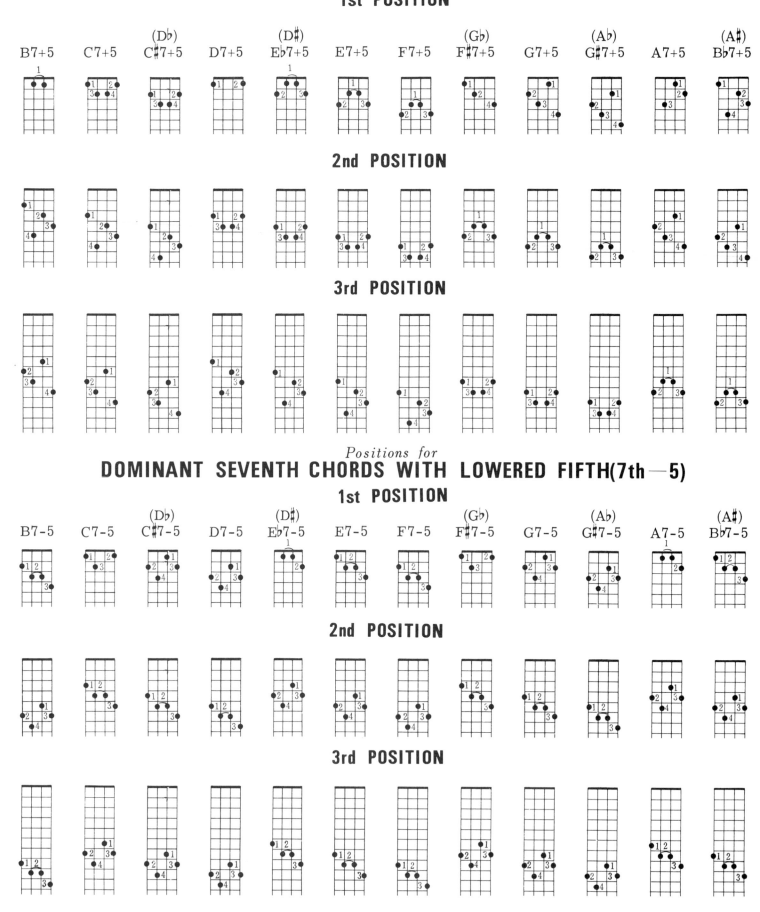

Positions for Major Seventh Chords

1st POSITION

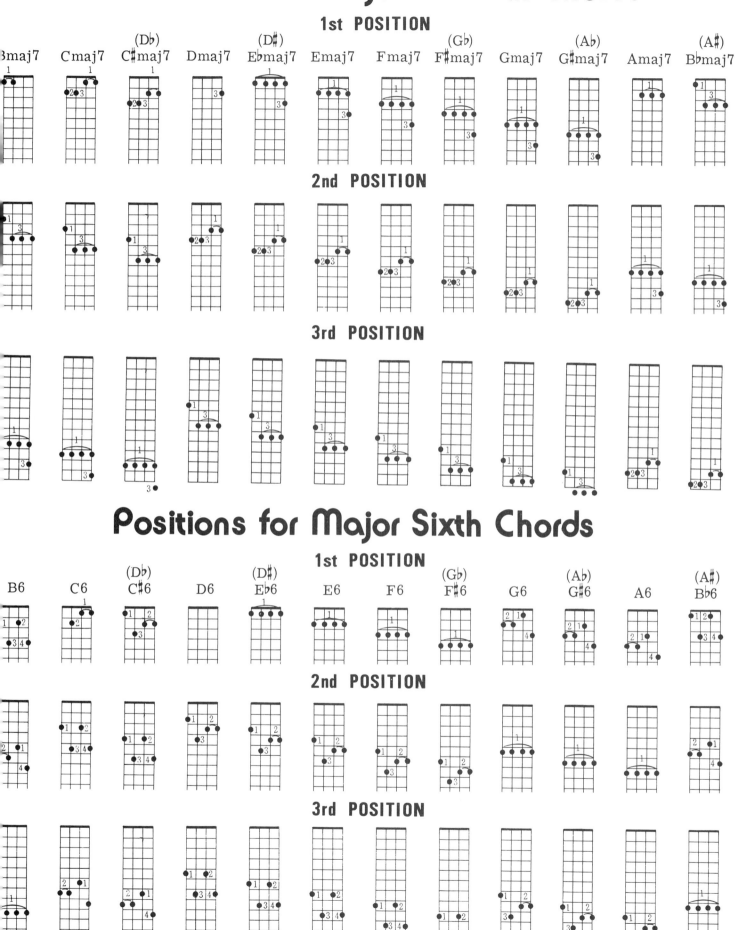

Bmaj7   Cmaj7   (Db) C#maj7   Dmaj7   (D#) Ebmaj7   Emaj7   Fmaj7   (Gb) F#maj7   Gmaj7   (Ab) G#maj7   Amaj7   (A#) Bbmaj7

2nd POSITION

3rd POSITION

Positions for Major Sixth Chords

1st POSITION

B6   C6   (Db) C#6   D6   (D#) Eb6   E6   F6   (Gb) F#6   G6   (Ab) G#6   A6   (A#) Bb6

2nd POSITION

3rd POSITION

Positions for
MINOR SEVENTH CHORDS
1st POSITION

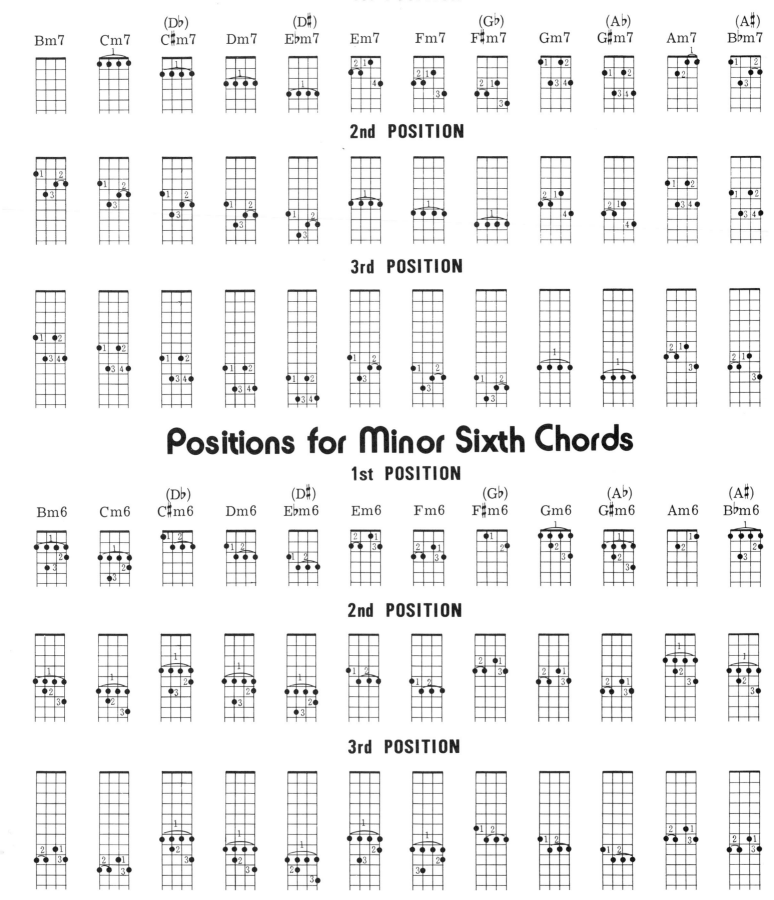

Positions for Minor Sixth Chords
1st POSITION